FRO

VANCOUVER PUBLIC LIBRARY

ARTISTRY in IRON

IRON

183 DESIGNS

EDITED BY

A. RAGUENET

DOVER PUBLICATIONS, INC.
MINEOLA, NEW YORK

Planet Friendly Publishing
✔ Made in the United States
✔ Printed on Recycled Paper
  Text: 10%   Cover: 10%
Learn more: www.greenedition.org

GREEN EDITION

At Dover Publications we're committed to producing books in an earth-friendly manner and to helping our customers make greener choices.

Manufacturing books in the United States ensures compliance with strict environmental laws and eliminates the need for international freight shipping, a major contributor to global air pollution.

And printing on recycled paper helps minimize our consumption of trees, water and fossil fuels. The text of *Artistry in Iron* was printed on paper made with 10% post-consumer waste, and the cover was printed on paper made with 10% post-consumer waste. According to Environmental Defense's Paper Calculator, by using this innovative paper instead of conventional papers, we achieved the following environmental benefits:

Trees Saved: 6 • Air Emissions Eliminated: 531 pounds
Water Saved: 2,558 gallons • Solid Waste Eliminated: 155 pounds

For more information on our environmental practices, please visit us online at www.doverpublications.com/green

Copyright

Copyright © 2010 by Dover Publications, Inc.
Electronic images copyright © 2010 by Dover Publications, Inc.
All rights reserved.

Bibliographical Note

This Dover edition, first published in 2010, contains a new selection of images from *Matériaux et documents d'architecture, de sculpture et des touts les arts industriels,* originally published in Paris, c. 1915. A CD-ROM containing all of the images has been included.

DOVER *Pictorial Archive* SERIES

This book belongs to the Dover Pictorial Archive Series. You may use the designs and illustrations for graphics and crafts applications, free and without special permission, provided that you include no more than ten in the same publication or project. (For permission for additional use, please write to Permissions Department, Dover Publications, Inc., 31 East 2nd Street, Mineola, N.Y. 11501.)

However, republication or reproduction of any illustration by any other graphic service, whether it be in a book or in any other design resource, is strictly prohibited.

Library of Congress Cataloging-in-Publication Data

Matériaux et documents d'architecture, de sculpture et des touts les arts industriels. Selections.
    Artistry in iron : 183 designs / edited by A. Raguenet. — Dover ed.
       p. cm. (Dover pictorial archive series)
    Originally published: Matériaux et documents d'architecture, de sculpture et des touts les arts industriels. Paris, c. 1915.
    Includes a CD-ROM containing all of the images.
    ISBN-13: 978-0-486-47398-7
    ISBN-10: 0-486-47398-8
     1. Ironwork—Pictorial works. I. Raguenet, A. II. Title.

NK8205.M282 2010
739.4—dc22
                                                                                    2009031886

DESIGN BY QUADRUM SOLUTIONS LTD.

Manufactured in the United States by Courier Corporation
47398801
www.doverpublications.com

NOTE

A rich and versatile supply of ornate architectural details, this collection of illustrations features decorative railings, balconies, candelabras, wrought-iron gates, and elaborate doorways. It showcases the diversity and enduring beauty of ironwork embellishments, a wondrous source of inspiration for artists, designers, and collectors.

Culled from a rare French multi-volume publication, these black-and-white images—superb examples of the ironworker's art—have been duplicated, combined, and artistically arranged to offer designers a wide range of creative possibilities. The accompanying CD-ROM contains both high- and low-resolution JPEG files of each page spread—exactly as shown in the book—and high- and low-resolution JPEG files of each individual motif.

The "Images" folder on the CD contains three different folders. All of the high-resolution image files have been placed in one folder, and the Internet-ready image files are in another folder. The third folder, "page spreads," contains two sub-folders: one holds all of the high-resolution JPEG files of the page spreads and the other holds the low-resolution JPEG files of the spreads. Every image has a unique file name in the following format: xxx.JPG. The first 3 digits of the file name, before the period, correspond to the number printed under the image in the book. The last 3 letters of the file name "JPG," refer to the file format. So, 001.JPG would be the first file in the folder.

Also included on the CD-ROM is Dover Design Manager, a simple graphics editing program for Windows that will allow you to view, print, crop, and rotate the images.

For technical support, contact:
  Telephone: 1 (617) 249-0245
  Fax: 1 (617) 249-0245
  Email: dover@artimaging.com
  Internet: http://www.dovertechsupport.com
  The fastest way to receive technical support is via email or the Internet.

001

001

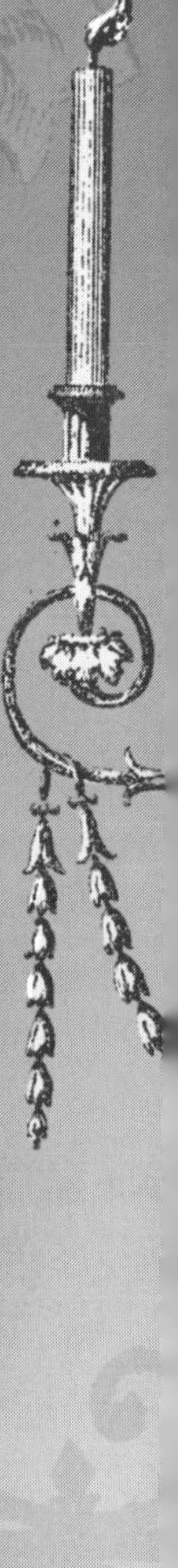

001

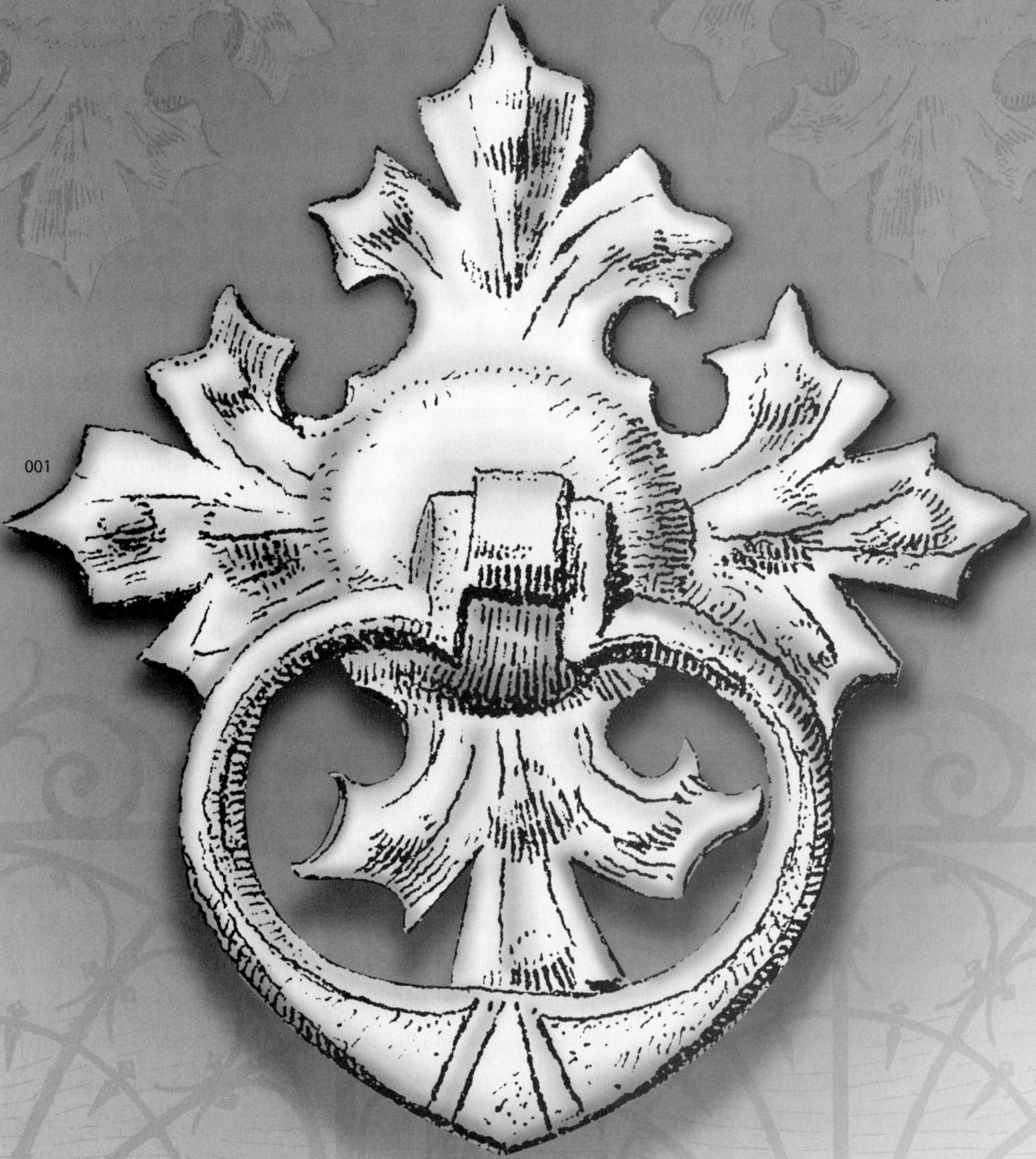

002

001

003

004

005

006

007

006

008

009

010

011

012

015

HOTEL

016

017

018

019

020

022

021

022

020

021

022

023

024

025

023

026

027

028

028

029

030

031

032

033

034

008

035

008

008

036

037

038

039

037

040

041

042

043

044

042

043

045

046

047

048

049

046

045

050

014

050

051

014

050

051

052

053

054

055

042

028

022

02

028

022

056

057

058

059

056

060

007

049

014

007

026

061

Chocolats DELACRE

063

062

013

008

051

008

064

057

065

066

057

065

067

068

069

008

051

069

070

071

072

073

074

007

007

007

007

074

007

005

075

076

023

077

005

078

079

080

080

081

082

083

082

006

085

086

087

088

089

090

091

091

092

088

093

042

007

042

094

095

096

097

098

099

096

007

007

013

100

100

042

101

102

103

104

105

094

105

106

057

107

108

109

022

110

110

111

112

113

016

114

113

036

115

036

AVE MARIA GRATIA PLENA DOMINVS TECVM BENEDICTA TV IN

116

117

118

119

120

057

045

004

121

122

017

057

073

123

124

123

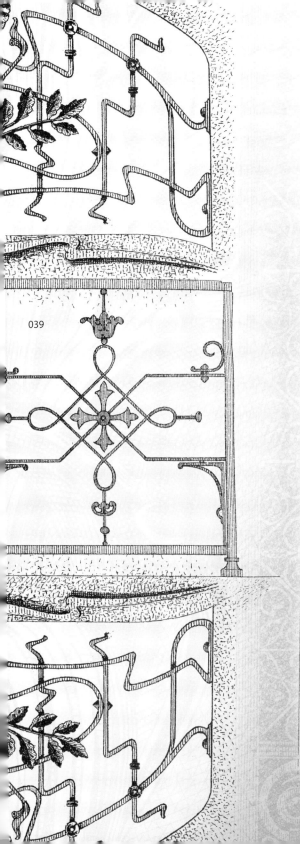

039

125

126

127

009

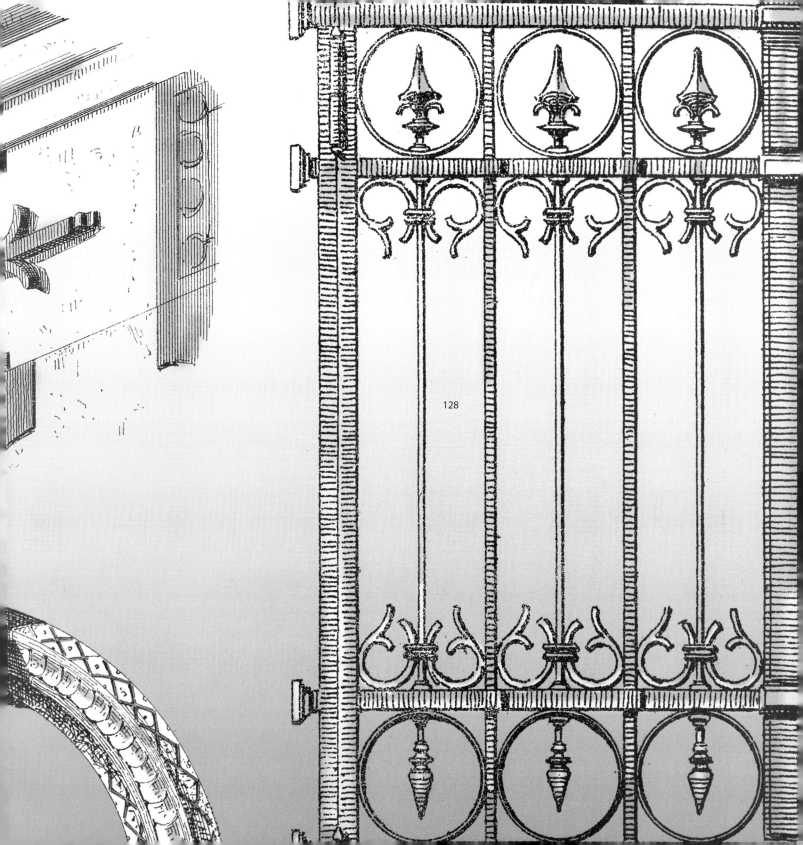

128

129

130

008

131

132

133

041

134

135

VIRTUTIS PRÆMIUM AVORVM

136

135

137

138

139

003

140

139

141

142

143

144

145

012

146

147

148

149

020

150

151

152

153

154

155

156

057

092

057

157

158

008

159

160

161

013

162

094

162

081

163

164

165

040

020

166

167

020

020

166

020

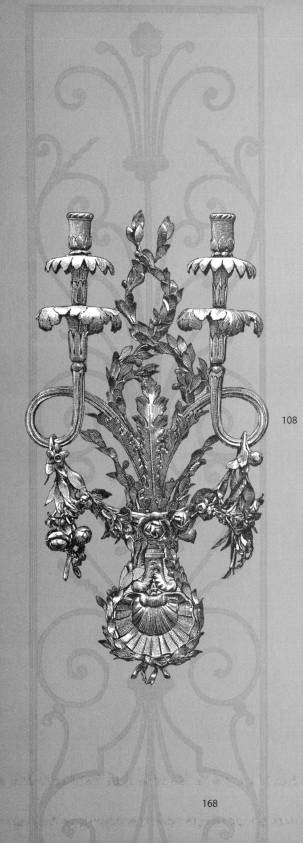

108

168

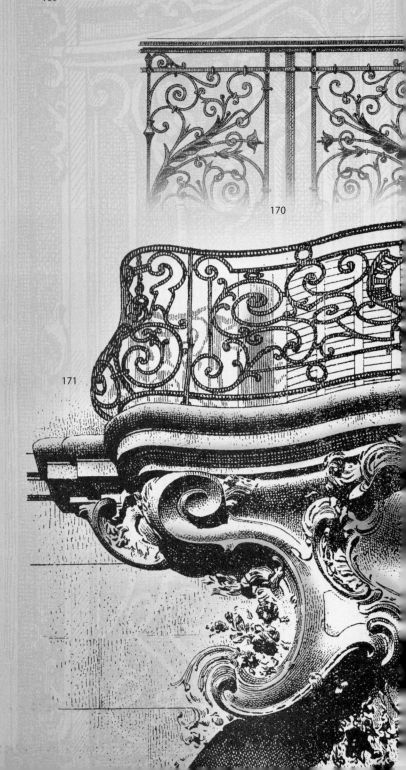

169

170

171

108

082

172

117

173

174

175

176

177

024

178

179

056

181

182

081

183

034

INDEX OF IMAGES

001

002

003

004

005

006

007

008

009

010

011

012

013

014

015

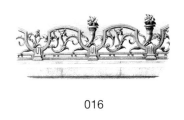

016

017

018

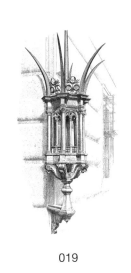

019

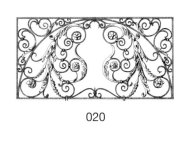

020

021

022

023

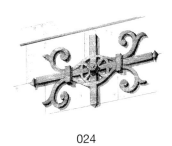

024

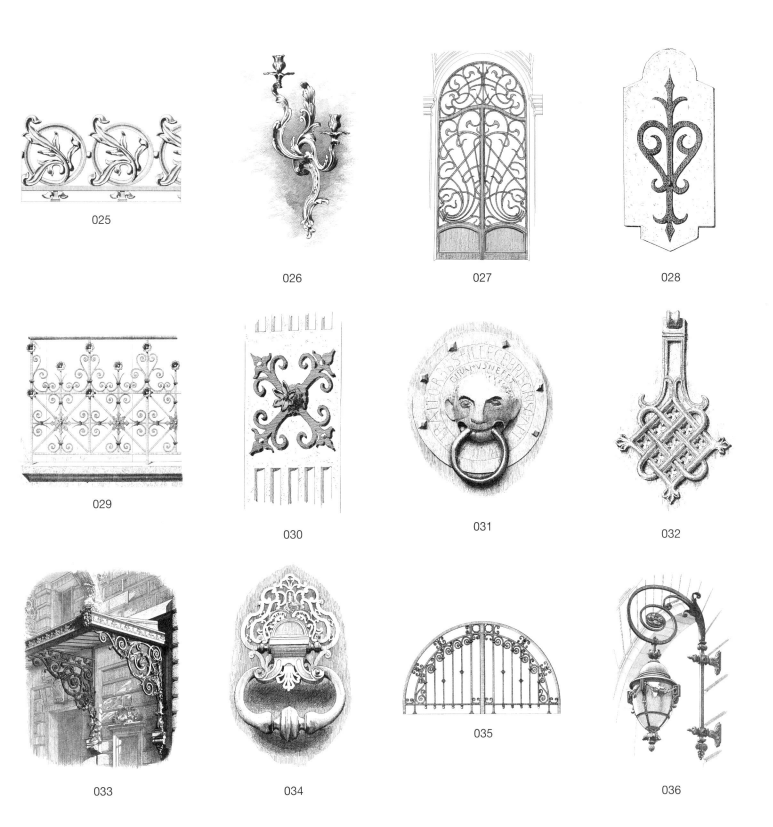

025

026

027

028

029

030

031

032

033

034

035

036

037

038

039

040

041

042

043

044

045

046

047

048

049

050

051

052

053

054

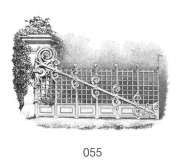

055

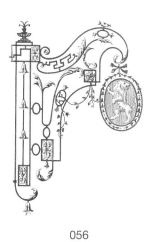

056

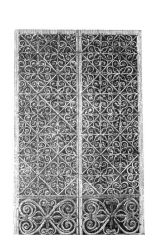

057

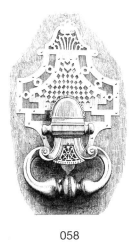

058

059

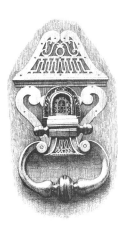

060

061

062

063

064

065

066

067

068

069

070

071

072

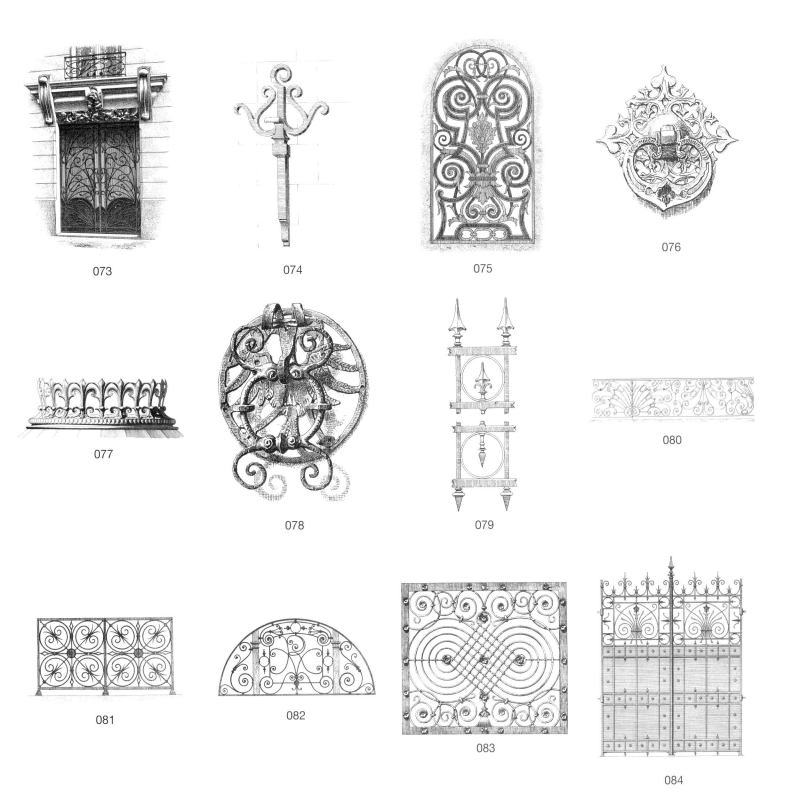

073

074

075

076

077

078

079

080

081

082

083

084

085

086

087

088

089

090

091

092

093

094

095

096

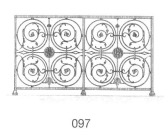

097

098

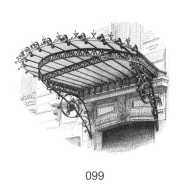

099

100

101

102

103

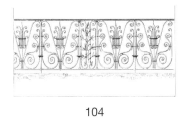

104

105

106

107

108

109

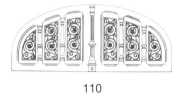

110

111

112

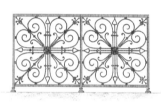

113

114

115

116

117

118

119

120

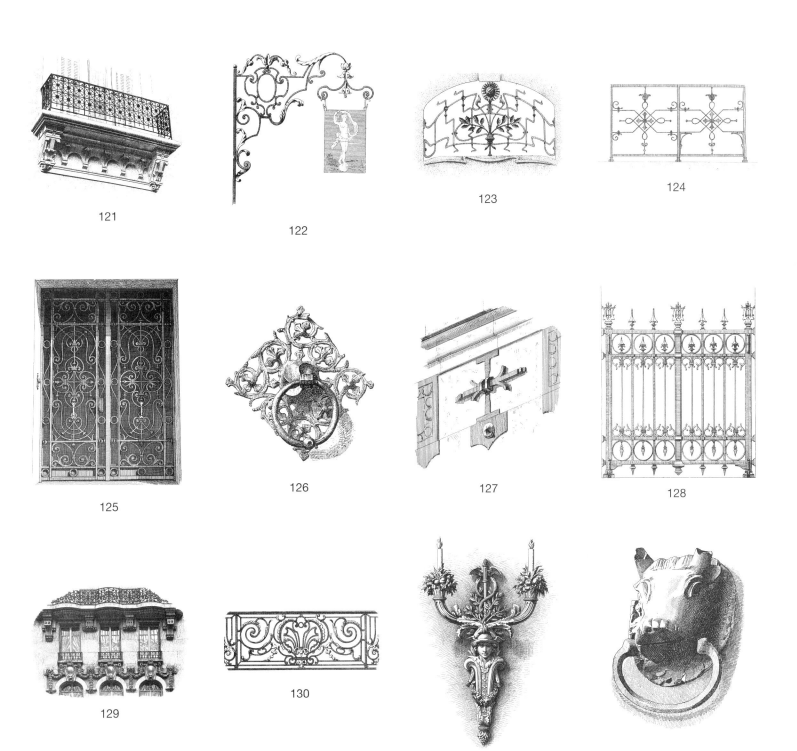

121

122

123

124

125

126

127

128

129

130

131

132

133

134

135

136

137

138

139

140

141

142

143

144

145

146

147

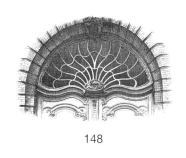

148

149

150

151

152

153

154

155

156

157

158

159

160

161

162

163

164

165

166

167

168

169

170

171

172

173

174

175

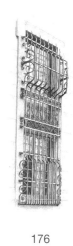

176

177

178

179

180

181

182

183